DÉCOUPAGE

This unusual grouping includes a child's antique wooden shoe tree découpaged with fine strips of floral border. A millefleurs glass vase adds to the Victorian theme. (Diane Dowe.)

DÉCOUPAGE

Kaye Healey

CRESCENT BOOKS
NEW YORK • AVENEL, NEW JERSEY

Previous page: This unusual grouping includes a child's antique wooden shoe tree découpaged with fine strips of floral border. A millefleurs glass vase adds to the Victorian theme. (Diane Dowe.)

Special thanks to découpeuse Diane Dowe for her assistance and advice.
Découpage: Diane Dowe, Laura Batalha, Stephen Wesgarth.
Wooden boxes made by Leonel Batalha.

This 1994 edition published by Crescent Books,
distributed by Outlet Book Company, Inc., a Random House Company,
40 Engelhard Avenue, Avenel, New Jersey 07001

Random House
New York • Toronto • London • Sydney • Aukland

First published in 1992
Reprinted in 1993
Reprinted in 1994

© Copyright Harlaxton Publishing Ltd
© Copyright design Harlaxton Publishing Ltd

Publishing Manager: Robin Burgess
Project Coordinator: Mary Moody
Editor: Dulcie Andrews
Illustrator: Kathie Baxter Smith
Designed & produced for the publisher by Phillip Mathews Publishers
Typeset in the U.K. by Seller's
Produced in Singapore by Imago

Title: Country Crafts Series: Découpage
ISBN: 0 517 08798 7

CONTENTS

A sumptuous wooden jewel case découpaged with prints of Persian and Coptic rugs is enhanced by hand-made beads. Note how a square picture has been cut in half and reversed to form the corners. (Diane Dowe.)

INTRODUCTION

Through this Country Craft series, it is our hope that you will find satisfaction and enjoyment in learning a new skill.

In this case, that of découpage. The decorative art of découpage is enjoying a well deserved revival of interest in many parts of the world. Mainly because this centuries-old craft, which is easy to learn, can transform the plainest of objects into beautiful pieces that can take their place beside family heirlooms.

Learning any new skill requires a little patience and practise and découpage is no exception. However, few pleasures compare with the satisfaction of making a beautifully crafted découpage piece, especially when it is admired by others and you can say 'I made it myself!'.

Découpage that is well crafted is in demand and this book will show you not only how to make lovely pieces for your own home or to give friends and relatives but, with practise, it could also be the means of earning extra income.

The photographs featured throughout this book show the decorative effects that can be created by placing découpage amongst 'sympathetic companion pieces' which will enhance their beauty. Part of the pleasure and fun of découpage (and it is fun) is entering into the world of fantasy and magic that it creates, and choosing where to place the finished object so that it will be a valued and treasured piece.

In this book you will find all the help you need to start creating your own unique piece of découpage.

GETTING STARTED

Before beginning, we should take a brief look at the fascinating history of découpage. Most crafts have evolved through the centuries by using materials which are readily available to create an object that is both functional and beautiful. Découpage is no exception to the rule.

History

The exact origins of the art of découpage are unknown. However early examples, now in museums and private collections throughout the world, reveal that it was used as a decorative art by many cultures such as the Chinese, Japanese, Persians and later, the Europeans. In England it was referred to as 'lacquering', 'Japanning' or 'lacquerware' and was much sought after. But it was the Italians who made découpage accessible in the 18th century, when hand-painted furniture was so fashionable that the demand could not be met by artisans.

The Venetians popularised découpage, which they called *l'arte del povero* meaning 'poor man's art'. Painstaking hand-painting by master craftsmen was substituted by apprentices who colored and cut fine engravings which were then applied to furniture to simulate a painting.

The craft flourished in Europe. England too was enamoured with the 'new' craze. So much so, that books such as the *Ladies' Amusement Book* featured designs by well-known artists fashioned exclusively for découpage. Its increasing popularity quickly moved it out of the milieu of the artisan and into ladies' drawing rooms to take its place beside embroidery as the fashionable pastime. So frenzied was the fashion at the court of Louis XVI, that original artworks are said to have been snipped up to embellish fans and screens! So don't feel guilty when you are about to take the scissors to cut your first picture from a book or magazine!

The term 'découpage' means 'cutting up' and usually, although not always, applies to paper.

Découpage Process

So what exactly is découpage? In very simple terms it is a process where pictures are cut out from books, posters, postcards or magazines and glued to objects or furniture, for example, boxes, tables, or trays. You can even use photographs or good quality laser photocopies, if they are correctly sealed. Layers of clear varnish are applied and sanded between coats. The finished product has the appearance of being handpainted and imbued with a rich, mellow glaze. Finally, it is polished with furniture polish or wax and buffed. You can découpage almost anything that has a smooth

Opposite: A selection of diverse objects suitable for découpage.
Almost anything with a smooth surface can be used.

A collection of designs in an array of colors and styles which will be used to découpage various items.

surface – glass, metal, wood, pottery, plaster – even eggs and rocks!

There are different schools of thought about découpage. The traditionalists adhere to 'the rules' and hand-color their pictures, often copies of old engravings, and apply twenty to fifty coats of varnish. Their work, no doubt, will be in the museums of the future.

Our approach will not be labor-intensive but will still produce a well finished and beautifully découpaged piece. With a little confidence and practise you can experiment and introduce different finishes and materials, once the basic principles are mastered.

Collecting Pictures

The first step is to begin collecting and sorting the pictures that will be used. These can be gleaned from many sources: forgotten boxes of greeting cards, old stamps on envelopes – even old letters, gift wrapping, theatre programmes, travel brochures, art exhibition or auction catalogs.

It is preferable to have in mind a theme or period for the piece that is going to be découpaged such as Victorian *millefleurs*, art nouveau, classical or modern, even humorous or 'grotesque'! We will come to these styles or periods a little later.

It is a good idea to gather together more pictures than you think will be needed for the project. There is nothing more frustrating than finding you do not have enough pictures when it comes to the layout. If one should be damaged in cutting or gluing, spares will prove invaluable.

Paper Thickness

The papers should be of a uniform thickness. The thickness of postcards, however, should not deter you from using them. Simply wet the card and carefully peel off the thicker layers of paper on the back and dry slowly, away from direct heat such as a stove, before cutting. If the paper is dried too quickly and at too intense a heat the paper may contract or wrinkle and be-come unusable.

Remember you are going to build up layers of varnish, therefore thicker paper will require many more coats until it blends into the object. For this reason it is best not to use thick and thin papers together but to try and use papers of uniform thickness to avoid an uneven surface. Indentations, valleys and ridges in which the varnish can build up will detract from the finished product.

Some magazine papers are not suitable because they are too thin and porous. Apart from the obvious problem of tearing, 'bleeding' can occur and the reverse may show through when they are glued down. This may not always occur, especially if the paper is sprayed or painted with a sealer before cutting and gluing. If you have a picture that you would like to use but are not sure if it will survive the 'bleeding' test – try it anyway. Some of the world's best discoveries have come from moments of daring!

Picture Definition

Pictures that are well defined will not only make cutting easier but they will have a sharper definition in the overall design.

Remember too, that faded or hazy pictures with very subtle coloring initially, such as old sepia prints, may end up looking quite in-distinct after many coats of varnish have been applied and they can lose their definition.

This could work in your favor if you wanted

a softer, old-world look. Pictures that look very bright or even garish at the outset will tone down and mellow under glaze.

Design Ideas

Ideas for the designs are limitless – although, you will probably want to start on something small and uncomplicated, until you have a 'feel' for the process and comfortable with it.

Beautiful boxes can be created using prints or postcards of old Persian or Oriental carpets and because of their rich but muted colors the application of layers of lacquer gradually builds up to emphasize the beauty of their antiquity. Découpage is very much a 'feeling' craft and the careful selection of a style or period will evoke this even more.

Our 'Beginner's Project' later in the book will show you how to get started using a step-by-step guide. Once you have découpaged your first piece, you will begin looking at books and magazines, not to say furniture, with a keener eye!

Different Materials

In this book we will be dealing mainly with paper. However, once the basics are mastered, you can go on to experiment with the technique and use other materials such as dried flowers, glitter, or even fabrics or sequins. Some sequins will lose their original color by chemically reacting with the varnish, so you will need to test such things before applying them to your work in progress. The possibilities are endless provided the material does not have an adverse chemical reaction.

Different finishes can be achieved by using products such as colored inks, pencils and paints or silver polish to give an 'antique' or weathered look. Gilding and burnishing are other treatments that can be used successfully with découpage.

The process is relatively simple, although like any craft it takes time to become familiar with the basics. Once this is done, your imagination has a free rein to experiment with other variations and combinations.

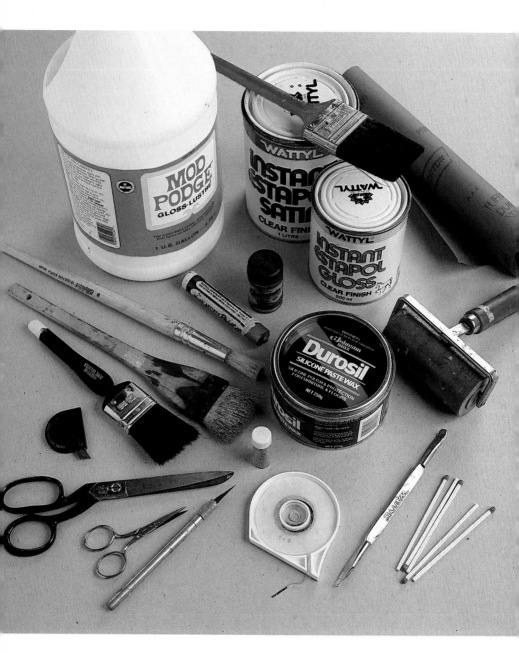

Basic tools to assist the découpage artist.

TOOLS AND MATERIALS

ART AND HOBBY supply stores now stock a comprehensive range of materials for the beginner as well as the professional. If in doubt about a product, ask the store manager for advice. Usually, they have art or craft experience themselves or have been dealing with the requirements of artists and craftspeople for some time. A hardware store will be the next stop.

The tools and materials needed for découpage are quite basic. However, items such as scissors and brushes should be the best you can afford. Nail scissors are not suitable as they are not fine enough. Embroidery or curved cuticle scissors will give a better edge especially when cutting into corners and curves. Long pointed scissors are also necessary. These tools, ideally, should be used exclusively for cutting découpage paper. A sharp craft knife or scalpel will give easier access to the intricacies of more difficult cuts.

A synthetic sable paintbrush with a chiselled edge will give a better finish and save frustration and disappointment later. A cheap paintbrush will shed hairs and spoil the finish. The size of the brush will depend on the object to be varnished. A 1 or 2 inch brush will be suitable to begin.

Some découpeurs like to use a small craft rubber roller to distribute the glue after the picture has been laid down but this is not essential. A soft cloth and wet sponge work equally well.

The list of basic requirements is as follows although you may not need all of these items initially:

- Scissors
  (long blades and cuticle or embroidery)
- Sharp craft knife or scalpel
- Brushes
- Tweezers
- PVA glue
  (water-soluble which dries clear)
- Fine wet and dry sandpaper
  and glass paper
- Clear gloss varnish
  plus mat or satin to finish
- Spray can of acrylic paint
- Sanding block
- Steel wool
- Paper tissues
- Soft clean cloths for dusting and polishing
- Fixative
- Mineral turpentine
- Sealer
- Wood filler acrylic primer or gesso
  (to smooth and finish wood surfaces)
- Re-usable adhesive
  (such as Bostik's Blu-Tack)
- Kitchen sponge (for wiping excess glue)

STARTING WORK

AN EYE FOR DETAIL will make all the difference to the finished product. Having decided on the item to be découpaged, the choice of print will be determined by the shape and size of the object.

Sources

Prints can be gathered from various sources; art books, available from museums and art gallery stores, or good quality magazines.

Remember that the paper should not be so thin that 'bleeding' can occur.

Special découpage picture books, available with reproductions of old lithographs, which can be hand-colored, if you would like to be more involved in creating a traditional affect.

Others feature the *millefleurs* style, which basically means a little of everything; flowers, dolls, bridges, boats, fans, urns, cameos, etc. These are glued in an overlapping fashion and completely cover the object resulting in a very Victorian look.

Old art books featuring Greek or Roman paintings, sculptures or architecture, particularly columns, are ideal for a classical theme; scrolls, garlands and birds for the Baroque period; and a mixture of the classical and humorous for the style known as 'grotesque'. Another, more adventurous and slightly difficult style is '*trompe l'oeuil*', a French term which means 'fool the eye'. This is the art of optical illusion, where larger and smaller scales are combined to create a picture with light and shadows painted into the scene giving an added dimension and perspective to the overall design.

Old books that have been damaged can be recycled with découpage and second-hand bookstores or book fairs sometimes offer an inexpensive source for pictures, particularly classical and Victorian. If the book is a little more expensive than hoped, simply divide the number of pictures you would use from it by the total price and work out how much each picture will cost. If you are going to découpage something very special the extra cost may be justified. If not, you could photograph or laser copy the ones you wanted and keep the book intact.

Filing

Gather the pictures together, preferably in a folder to prevent damage to the print. As you become more involved with the craft of découpage you will want to keep groups of pictures in their own categories. This will make the selection of images for a new piece much easier. Plastic folders or sleeves, available from stationery stores, are convenient ways to catalog the groups. As your interest expands you will probably move up to a regular filing cabinet!

Opposite: A box exquisitely découpaged inside and out. (Diane Dowe.)

An old wooden chair has been given a new lease of life. (Diane Dowe.)

Work Area

Try to have a designated craft work area if possible. A place that has good natural light, adequate ventilation and is relatively dust-free. A comfortable chair and easy access to all materials will make découpage a pleasure eagerly anticipated. Ideally, it should be a place where you will not have to keep packing everything away after use, although, if there are small children or animals in the household, this will have to be a consideration.

A child's wooden case découpaged onto a red background using Mickey Mouse cut-outs from a child's old encyclopedia. (Wooden case by Leonel Batalha. Découpage by Diane Dowe.)

A turn-of-the-century hat box découpaged in the Renaissance style with Madonnas from an architecture magazine. With this is a tall, glass cylinder done in an all-over millefleurs style. (Diane Dowe.)

TECHNIQUES OF THE CRAFT

THE BASIC TECHNIQUES for creating a beautiful piece of découpage are not difficult to learn. With patient practise, you will develop the skills to master this creative craft.

This chapter explains in detail the techniques needed both to prepare the surface ready for work and then to carry out the stages involved in the process of découpage.

Preparing the Surface

If the surface is slightly irregular to begin with, you may have to paint it with acrylic primer or gesso before you commence. These products are readily available at art supply stores and simple to use. Applied in smooth strokes along the grain, they cover the grain and fill in any ridges or bumps in the wood, providing a smooth surface on which to paint a background or glue pictures. If the surface is smooth to start with, then you need not use gesso.

When dry, sand the surface lightly with a wet and dry sandpaper until it is smooth. Buff with fine steel wool, then dust it thoroughly. Now the surface is ready.

Next, you have a choice between painting an all-over background color with an acrylic paint, or covering the box, tray or other object with prints or paper so that none of the original surface shows. The choice is yours.

Whether you plan to cover the object with paint or paper, apply a coat of varnish over the surface to seal it.

You will need to wait for 12 to 24 hours, depending on drying conditions. The varnish must be dry before gluing. Allow it to dry naturally. Do not be tempted to speed up the process with a hair dryer or a heater.

If a new wooden item is being used such as a small box, you may have to remove the hinges or clasps before you begin. But be warned – it may be difficult to get them back on again after the build-up of the layers of paper and varnish. It may be easier to spend a little more time working around them and leaving them in place.

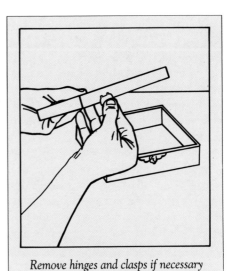

Remove hinges and clasps if necessary to make varnishing easier.

Painting the background of a small box.

Removing Bubbles

If the glue is applied to the paper background while it is still damp, bubbles can form under the picture. If this occurs at any stage of the process, do not panic! Simply wait until the picture is dry and using either a pin or a fine scalpel, make a small hole or incision and add glue, a drop at a time, then press the edges gently together. Try and make the cut in an inconspicuous place, just in case there are complications.

A soft colored pencil or felt-tip pen can camouflage minor cutting errors especially if some background has been left on the print. This is where the importance of careful and accurate cutting will be appreciated. Go around edges carefully, perhaps moistening the pencil with the tip of your tongue.

Please note: this should only be done when the glue on the pictures has dried, otherwise smudging or tearing may result.

Sealing

All prints should be sealed with a varnish on both sides before cutting and gluing. Paint one side first and when dry, turn over and paint the other side. If you have space, you may be able to put up a miniature clothes line with small pegs, as used in a photographer's darkroom, to hang the pictures while they are drying. This would enable you to seal both sides at the same time. Alternatively, you can use a spray fixative as a sealer, if you prefer.

If you decide to seal with a paintbrush and varnish, remember to stir the contents well; stir slowly to avoid air bubbles. Dip the brush into the varnish and wipe carefully against the lip of the can and apply the loaded side of the brush to the paper. Use smooth even strokes in one direction and avoid dust and foreign objects getting onto the wet varnish. When the papers are dry, cutting can commence. If the cutting is done first, before

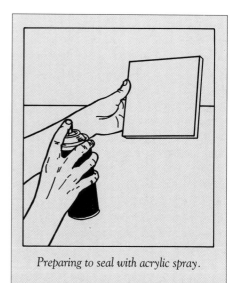

Preparing to seal with acrylic spray.

A small Victorian scrap-screen has been découpaged using photographs from an original and valuable scrapbook. The picture has a floral garland of similar photographs. (Diane Dowe.)

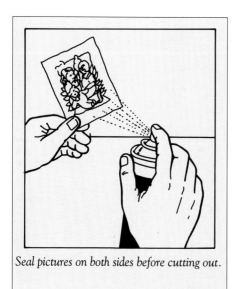

Seal pictures on both sides before cutting out.

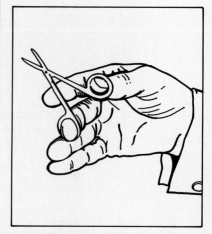

Hold scissors in a relaxed manner.

the varnish is applied, there is a chance the picture could curl which could make gluing down the prints more difficult.

Cutting

Now to commence cutting. This is a vital part of the process. Patience and attention to detail are now of the utmost importance. Hold the paper in your left hand (or right if you are left-handed) and let it flow in a fluid movement through the scissors as they cut. Relax and allow the paper to move freely but do not push it. The pointed blades should curve out away from the paper and the points of the scissors should never close completely on the paper. Otherwise an unsightly tear or ragged edge will spoil the picture.

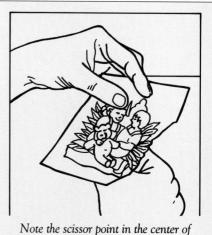

Note the scissor point in the center of the white area at the beginning of detailed cutting.

Opposite: A turn-of-the-century tin top-hat box and violin case are découpaged in the millefleurs style using sheet music. A simple wooden box is transformed using an illuminated manuscript art print. (Hat box by Diane Dowe. Violin case by Laura Batalha).

An 18th century tapestry print shows how one picture can be used to cover an entire box.
(Wooden box by Leonel Batalha. Découpage by Diane Dowe.)

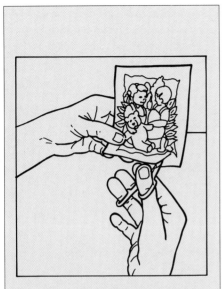

Feed the paper through the scissors.

The objective is to guide and cut the paper as evenly as possible without leaving any corners or sharp edges. This is where the embroidery or cuticle scissors are invaluable for smooth curves. Long-bladed scissors should only be used on the straight cutting edges. Corners need special care, especially when cutting into a 'v' or around filigree.

Accurate and careful cutting is one of the most important parts of découpage and a little patience here will bring rewards later.

When cutting around an image such as a bouquet of flowers or an intricate tree, cut off the excess as you go, otherwise it will pull down on the paper making a good cut difficult. If the cutting is very delicate and detailed, it is a good idea to leave fretwork or 'bridges' of paper connected to the picture to give extra stability. These can be cut away last.

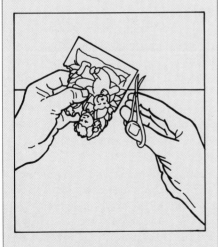

Only the paper moves.

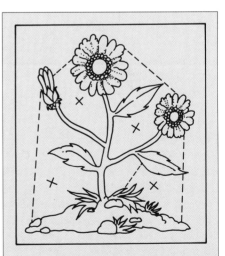

Leave 'fretwork' or bridges of paper until last to cut, as it will support the paper, making cutting intricate details easier.

As each picture is cut out, position it on the box or item to be découpaged until the overall effect is achieved. Fix the pictures into place temporarily with re-usable adhesive to see how they fit the layout and the object. Take your time and do not be concerned yet about gluing or varnishing. Just move the pieces around until they fit the space and look harmonious. Remember that the end result is going to look like a simulated hand-painted piece so, unless an overall *millefleurs* style is desired, a sparser effect is better.

Place all sealed prints in a flat folder until you need to use them.

Gluing

When the prepared surface is completely dry, apply the water-soluble glue to the surface where the picture is to be positioned, then to the picture and paste the picture down.

Use your finger to spread the glue on the surface. This will help find any recalcitrant bumps too. Always put the glue on the item to be découpaged as well as the print so that an even bonding is achieved between paper and the surface of the object.

Be generous with the glue but carefully wipe any excess away with a soft damp kitchen sponge (cut into small squares for easy handling). If the paper is fine be a little cautious so that it does not tear or dislodge. All traces of glue should be removed before the next coat of varnish is applied, otherwise you can end up with brown smudges on the finished product. Water and a little vinegar will help remove stubborn glue spots.

Press the paper using a cloth or roll with a small craft roller to distribute the glue evenly

Applying glue to the surface.

and insure there are no air bubbles remaining under the paper.

Have a wet cloth and a towel nearby for wiping the glue from your hands and rinse it out often.

Picture edges are important. Insure they are well glued and firmly applied. If not, the next picture to be glued may lift them. Also there is a danger that varnish can seep in underneath the picture and cause an unsightly bulge.

If the picture is not quite centered, use the tweezers to gently lift and reposition it. Glue down larger pictures as you would apply wallpaper, taking care not to stretch the paper as you lay it down on the glued surface.

Continue in this way until the object is covered with your design.

This commedia dell'arte miniature theatre is an instant 'set' on a bow-legged occasional table. The table has been découpaged using a sheet of floral gift wrapping. The document box is découpaged with oriental rugs. (Table by Stephen Westgarth. Document box by Diane Dowe.)

An unusual collection of 'found' objects with a tall, golden gourd decorated in the millefleurs style. The picture frame in the background is découpaged using black paint and gold dust. (Gourd by Laura Batalha. Frame by Diane Dowe.)

Varnishing

Now we come to the application of the varnish. There are several schools of thought on how many coats are desirable. Only you can decide when you think there are enough. However, three to ten coats is usually regarded as a minimum guide (depending on the thickness of the papers and the varnish) before commencing sanding, otherwise there is a danger the print could be damaged if it is too close to the surface A professional découpeur might not begin sanding until forty coats have been applied!

Each coat should be applied in alternate directions and allowed to dry overnight or for 24 hours, depending on the weather.

Again, a little care is needed. Brush-strokes should always be in one direction and will alternate between coats; i.e. north to south for one coat – dry – east to west for the next and so on. Try to develop a rhythm and flow when painting so the varnish will be applied in smooth, even strokes. You will no doubt have newspaper underneath to keep the area clean but watch that the varnish does not dribble down the exterior and stick to the newspaper to form an unsightly ridge of varnish around the base. A good handy hint is to mark an arrow on the newspaper with a felt-tipped pen or pencil showing in which direction you are painting. If you are interrupted by a caller or the telephone, you will know where you were when you began.

Clean the brush well and dry it on a cloth, as excess turpentine on the brush can make sections of the varnish thinner in some areas. A uniform application of varnish is the aim.

Between coats, the varnish brush should be placed in a container of turpentine. Some découpeurs use a baby's glass feeding bottle

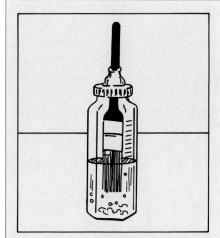

Your brush should be suspended in turpentine between coats of varnish. A baby's bottle is a good container because it keeps the brush away from contaminating sediment.

which has the rubber teat cut at the top and the handle of the brush inserted through it. This enables the brush to hang suspended in the turpentine and not pick up the sediment at the bottom of the bottle. Clean brushes are an absolute necessity and this idea can save time and messy cloths.

Good conditions are essential – a dust-free zone, adequate ventilation and good lighting. If the weather is very wet or humid the drying process will take longer. Do not be tempted to rush at this point as 'blooming' or cloudiness can occur.

Also, avoid sunlight which can damage découpage at any stage. Between coats rest the varnished piece on four or six paper cups which have been turned upside down. This

Classically découpaged boxes sit on top of aminiature oak chest of drawers.
(Wooden box by Leonel Batalha. Découpage by Diane Dowe.)

provides a level surface and allows the air to circulate which aids the drying process.

Sanding

Depending on the thickness of the paper and of the varnish, when three to ten coats or more have been applied and the découpage is dry to the touch, sanding can commence. It is always difficult to decide when to begin sanding and it is something that comes with experience. Initially, it is better to apply more coats rather than fewer. No damage can be done that way.

Use a fine, wet and dry sandpaper that has been dipped in water and wrap it around the sanding block. Put a few drops of water on the découpage and begin sanding lightly, in the same direction. A few drops of detergent can be added to a small bowl of water and this will make the harder sanding a little easier.

Try to maintain an even pressure while sanding. What you are doing now is levelling out the bumps and ridges and making a smooth, even surface.

When the varnish is completely dry, dust carefully with a lint-free cloth and apply another coat. Do not worry if the surface looks cloudy when this is being done as this is quite normal. Remember that the object of the exercise is to gradually build up the varnish so the edges of the cut paper blend into the surface and an inlaid effect is achieved.

When the surface is dry, wipe with a damp lint-free cloth to remove any dust. Dust on wet paint produces a gritty effect which spoils the finished product. Continue with another ten coats or more, in this way; varnish, allow to dry for 24 hours or until dry to the touch, sand and dust.

Always clean and suspend brushes in turpentine after each application. Change it regularly and rinse out the bottle so that it is free of sediment. Insure the varnish can is tightly capped after use. Always stir varnish before use, but never shake the tin as this will cause air bubbles.

Inside and Underside Surfaces

The insides and undersides of boxes are as important as the exteriors. An exquisitely découpaged piece with a neglected interior detracts from all the good work that has gone into it. You can choose between continuing the découpage inside the lid, lining with a suitable paper or fabric, or if it has a beautiful grain leave it the way it is. There are many elegant gift wrappings or Japanese rice papers that can be cut to measure and glued to the interior. Fabrics such as silk, satin, taffeta, felt, fine velvet or Liberty prints are suitable.

Some découpeurs cut and cover card inserts which are glued to the in-sides of boxes. These inserts can also be padded with a thin, flat batting – not quilting as it is too thick and bulky.

Lining with Fabric

Lining a box should be left until the découpage is finished. Dust, water, glue or varnish will end up on the inside of the box at some stage no matter how careful you are.

To line a box with fabric requires that the fabric be backed, as you cannot glue straight onto the inside of the box. A lightweight card such as shirt card is suitable. Measure the inside base of the box and cut the card to match. Trim off about 3/16 inch all round.

Place the card template on the wrong side of the material you are going to use and cut the material 1/2 inch larger than the card.

Cut off the corners of the material to the edge of the card. This forms a neat, mitered corner when it is glued down on the wrong side. Glue all edges of the card and fold the material over the glued sides. The base piece is measured and cut first, then the sides. Each piece should be measured and covered one at a time.

If all the pieces are cut out at once, measuring only the first piece, they may not be accurate due to the thickness of the card and of the material when it is folded and pasted. The inside top of the box can be treated in the same manner if it is suitable for lining in this way. Alternatively, it could be painted with gold paint or burnished with gold leaf.

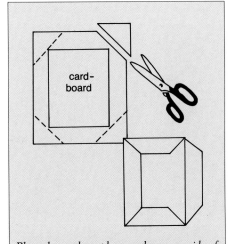

card-
board

Place the card template on the wrong side of the material and cut the corners to the edge of the card. This is called a 'miter' and it eliminates the bulk of the material when it is folded over and glued.

FINISHING TECHNIQUES

NOW we come to the final one or two coats to finish off the découpage. At this stage you can add any of these finishing touches – gold crayon, gold dust, sequins, self-adhesive gold tape or little stars.

Special Effects

Gold dust will be easier to use if you mix it into a little of the varnish and paint it onto selected areas, such as the lip or edge of a box. Otherwise it will be difficult to get it to stay in the areas where you want it. (*Note:* the item to be découpaged should be completely dry before these touches are applied.)

Use these touches subtly and selectively or your découpage may end up looking clumsy and garish.

Gold crayon can be used to good effect around the edges. Sequins and gold stars can be applied in the same way as gold dust but remember some colors may interact with the chemicals in the varnish and change their color.

Peel off the adhesive backing of the self-adhesive gold tape and apply by pressing your thumb nail along the tape. A good eye is needed to insure the line is straight, perhaps by lightly drawing a fine line first, which the gold tape will cover.

Once your finishing touches have been applied, prior to the last few coats of varnish, the sandings should be lighter, otherwise you could sand through to the gold.

The Final Coat

Whether you choose any of the special effects or not, you will still need to decide if you want a gloss or mat finish for the final coat of your découpaged object.

A small tin of varnish of your choice and preferably a new brush is needed for this penultimate and important process.

Sand again as previously and apply the finish in smooth, even strokes in the same direction. Hold the découpage to the light to insure a complete coverage.

Depending on your disposition, the final treatment with furniture polish or a light wax will be either a tedious chore or a labor of love!

Using a soft cloth and a small amount of polish, wax or paste, apply to small areas, a little at a time, and buff before it sets hard. Some découpeurs find that warming the polish or paste first speeds up the process by spreading the polish more easily.

It will take six months or more until the découpage has fully 'cured' to a rock-hard surface. Even so, it will always need to be handled with care as, like fine china, it can chip if dropped or knocked against a hard object.

Opposite: A simple wooden tray, découpaged in the 1960s using a wreath pattern.
An example of how functional and durable découpage can be. (Diane Dowe.)

During this period, polish the piece regularly. If not each day, then once a week. This will bring out the deep, mellow tones and help give the découpage an 'antique' feeling. The surface should be as smooth as ivory or satin to the touch and very tactile.

A contemporary screen découpaged with old 1960's and 70's New Yorker magazine covers. A good example of grouping sympathetic companion pieces. (Diane Dowe.)

BEGINNER'S PROJECT

NOW that we have covered the basic procedures of découpage let us start on the first project. We are not going to be overly ambitious with this one. Choose a small object that will not take too long to complete so you can be sufficiently inspired by your accomplishment to go on and experiment with other projects that are a little more ambitious.

We are going to découpage a small and inexpensive oval box which was bought from a hobby store. Most hobby stores stock boxes in a good range of sizes. They come in many shapes: square, round, long, heart-shaped and hexagonal, to name a few. They do not require much preparatory work – just a light sanding with a fine sandpaper.

MATERIALS

Sandpaper
Small paintbrush
Hobby or craft glue
Small sharp scissors
Magazines of your choice for pictures
Spray can of black acrylic paint
Can of gloss varnish
Small rubber roller from hobby store
Stencil knife or scalpel

If you want to add a touch of elegance buy some gold dust and gold self-adhesive tape at the hobby store.

You will also need a little patience and care for the first project.

Now you are ready to start.

METHOD
Step One
Lightly sand the exterior of the box and brush away the wood dust. Wipe with a soft, clean, lint-free cloth. Eradicating dust is most important, otherwise it will mingle with the paint and create a gritty surface. This seems like a small and obvious point and one we come back to constantly but it is essential to keep dust and hair away from the surface.

Opposite: An example of selective découpaging. The lid of this cigar box has been decorated in a classical all over style. The rest of the box features cigar labels. What man could resist such a gift! (Diane Dowe.)

Right: A plywood box in its raw state being prepared for the first stage of sanding.

Center: The same box after an initial coat of acrylic black paint which will form the background for the découpage.

Far right: The completed project — a small Victorian-style decorative box gilded with gold dust and gold tape.

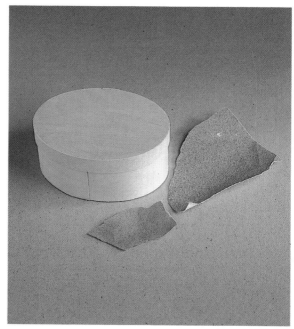

Step Two

Find a place outdoors that is free from dust, where you can spread out newspapers and spray the box. Place the top and bottom of the box facedown to avoid getting paint on the inside. Spray the exterior with the black acrylic spray paint. Make a good start by spraying it evenly.

It is better to give two light coats with drying time in between, than one heavy one that may result in paint build-up or runs. Bring the work inside when it is dry.

Step Three

This is where you will show your own creative individuality. Select the pictures you need to decorate the box. Our first project is a motif style. That means that the box will not be entirely covered with pictures but will contain a number of picture arrangements. Select pictures with a theme. You might have medals, buttons, antique furniture or flowers. Give some thought to color too. It is best if the picture looks rich and appealing against the black background. The empty spaces are as important in the overall design as the covered areas. So you will need to decide which areas of the box you will want to cover.

Now select a quiet place where there is good light. Seal all the pictures on both sides

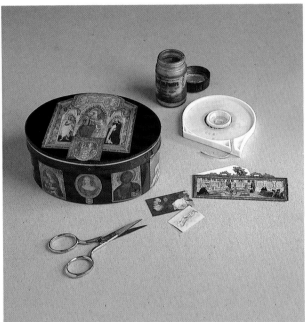

with varnish. This is a very important step as the glue may seep through from below and cause bubbles if a protectant is not applied. Leave to dry before cutting out, using either small, sharp, curved or long scissors, carefully cut out the pictures. Work slowly around essential details such as a nose or the delicate shape of a flower and try to get smooth, rounded edges – not jagged ones. Remember that the cut picture, with any flaws, will be highlighted against the black background. Now lay out the pictures on the box. How do they look? Do you need more – or less?

Step Four

Apply the glue to the back of the picture and the box itself. Make sure there is adequate coverage. Set down the pictures on the box, using tweezers if necessary, and roll them flat with the roller to get rid of air bubbles. Wipe away any excess glue. Although the glue is white now that it is wet, it will dry clear. Do not découpage the lip of the box because it will not close properly and your work will be obscured anyway. Continue pasting down the images until you are satisfied that the box is the way you want it to look. The overall effect will be much better if the bottom of the box is découpaged too. But wait until the sides are dry before attempting to turn it over to do that part.

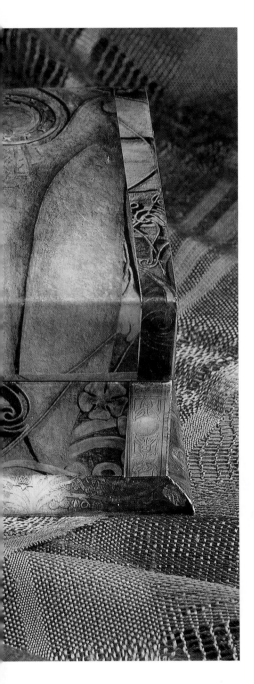

A rich gold and green box découpaged in an
ecclesiastical style.
(Wooden box by Leonel Batalha.
Découpage by Diane Dowe.)

Step Five

When the box is dry to the touch you can commence varnishing. This box will need about six coats of varnish because it is only a decorative box. One that is in constant use, such as a jewelry box or a document box, will need many more coats – as many as twenty coats. The next stage is all about technique and is very important. Take the brush and dip it into the varnish smoothly and slowly. (You will, of course, have stirred the varnish beforehand and allowed it to settle so there are no air bubbles). Draw the brush against the lip of the can to remove excess varnish from one side only. Lay the full side of the brush against the top of the box first and use long, smooth strokes to cover the surface. Do not overlap but lay one stroke of varnish next to the last stroke.

Avoid drips down the side of the box. If they do occur, carefully wipe them away with a clean cloth. Also avoid creating rough edges on the box by positioning it so the wet varnish does not touch your work area.

Perhaps you would like to try balancing it on the upturned paper cups mentioned previously or you could place it on clean matches. Choose what suits you best. When completely covered, leave in a dust-free place away from children and animals. Hair can so easily ruin a glazed surface. It is dry when it is smooth to the touch and cannot be marked by a fingernail. Apply three coats of varnish in this manner. If air bubble develop you are neither dipping nor applying the varnish correctly. This part of the procedure requires concentration and attention to detail.

Step Six

After three coats of varnish you will begin to see how beautiful it is going to look – but this is only the beginning! Now you have to sand the surface lightly to make it as perfect as you can. If you look closely, you will see irregularities such as air bubbles, uneven build-up of varnish, drips and scratches. Wipe the sanded box carefully. Do not worry if it looks 'cloudy' as that is caused by the sanding.

You could continue with another three coats of varnish, sanding in between each coat or at this point, you could add any decorative finishes using the gold dust or self-adhesive tape. Add some gold dust to a small amount of varnish in a separate container. Use a clean brush to apply to a specific area, such as the lip of the box. Be subtle – it is easy to 'gild the lily' and spoil the effect. Use the self-adhesive gold tape on the edge of the box as a border. It lifts easily enough for you to experiment with the positioning.

When you are happy with the way it looks, press it into place with the back of your fingernail. You can use it on gentle curves too, as seen in the black Victorian scrap-screen. Allow at least a day to dry and then polish the box with furniture wax to complete your first project in découpage.

INDEX

—